How Successful People Think Differently

Akash P. Karia

http://AkashKaria.com

#1 Bestselling Author of
"Ready, Set...Procrastinate! 23 Anti-Procrastination Tools
Designed to Help You Stop Putting Things Off and
Start Getting Things Done"

PRAISE FOR "HOW SUCCESSFUL PEOPLE THINK DIFFERENTLY"

"This book is packed with really wonderful mind sets, reframes, and psychology tips, all backed with references and real science. *I love the way the information was presented and the tips themselves are super powerful. This is like the "best of the best" self help tips. Very highly recommended! A quick read, but a thanksgiving feast of food for thought."*

— *Tim Brennan, Author of 1001 Chess Tactics*

*"How Successful People Think Differently is a quick, easy read packed with practical tips and easy-to-follow advice...*This book is for anyone who wants to aim higher.*"*

— *Gillian Findlay*

"This is a good book for many people who are still clinging to the fence, procrastinating and not achieving their goals. *I highly recommend it!"*

— *Allan Kaufman, DTM, MBA*

"Just when I thought I knew about everything, along comes this book. *It is a great non fiction book filled with many useful tips…"*

— *William Leland*

"**Great, easy to digest tips you can act on immediately, tip by tip or all at once.** *I highly recommend reading this book if you want to create success in your life.*"

—*Karen W*

"*I was pleasantly surprised that I learned new tips from this book.* **It gave me great ideas on how to think differently and put tips into place to change habits** *and create a more successful life.*"

— *Stacy Nichols*

"*...incredibly useful book* **filled with scientifically backed advice** *on how to successfully reach your goals.*"

— *Ryan Berd*

"*This short and deceptively simple book contains a distillation of many other self-help and 'success literature' books...Illustrated by many examples from real life and generously filled with scientific references and suggestions for further reading,* **this book is a 'must have' for anyone who wishes to better themselves in life – no matter what the goal may be.**"

— *John Joyce, Author of "Masterpiece"*

"**...no filler, no fluff – just the absolutely necessary information peppered with some great stories and practical examples.** *It is a quick read and a no-nonsense guide to making a lasting change in one's life.*"

— *Mandy Hoffeldt*

CONTENTS

To Mum and Dad,

Nisha and Paresh Karia,

For all that I am

Or ever hope to be,

I owe to you.

YOUR FREE GIFT

As a way of saying thank you for your purchase, I'd like to offer you a free bonus package worth $297. This bonus package contains eBooks, videos and audiotapes on how to overcome procrastination, master the art of public speaking and triple your productivity. You can download the free bonus here: http://AkashKaria.com/FREE/

CHAPTER ONE

UNLOCKING THE
SCIENCE OF SUCCESS

*"One can have no smaller or greater mastery than
mastery of oneself."*

—Leonardo da Vinci

Why is it that some people are able to achieve so much success - in their personal, professional, social lives - whereas so many others are struggling?

For example, when two people commit to a goal - say, to go to the gym and lose weight, why does one of them manage to follow through, and the other one doesn't?

What is the successful person doing differently (whether it's losing weight, starting a business or learning a new skill) from the failures?

Are successful people wired differently from the rest of us? Is success simply encoded in their DNA? Or is it something else?

1

Is it formal education?

No, there are thousands of broke, unemployed, unhappy people with doctorates and there are thousands of rich, happy people with only a high-school education.

Yes, formal education is important, but through my research I have found that lack of a degree does not equal lack of success. As long as you have a basic high school diploma, and you're willing to invest in yourself by reading books and listening to audiotapes, you possess enough education to be successful in life. Never let the lack of a degree be an excuse for a lack of success in your life.

Well is it intelligence? Again, there are thousands of people who're earning millions of dollars, who're in happy relationships and have great health even though they are less intelligent than you. These are people who graduated in the half of the class that made the top half...possible. There is nothing quite as frustrating as seeing someone who is dumber than you making more money than you.

So, if it's not education and its not intelligence that makes the difference between successful people and unsuccessful people, what exactly is it?

And the more important question is: How can we get access to the magic ingredient that successful people have and add it to our own lives so that we too may experience more success in our lives?

Until the last 100 years or so, we didn't really have a concrete answer to these questions.

There were lots of theories, there were a lot of books, and anyone and everyone had their own opinion. Your best bet until recently was to go to an unsuccessful person, ask them their theories on success...and then do the exact opposite!

However, in the last 100 years, science has made remarkable progress in unlocking the secrets behind success. Unfortunately, a lot of this great, life-changing research is hidden inside dense, boring, hard-to read academic literature.

Fortunately, I've gone through that research for you - and in this booklet, you're going to be getting access to life-changing tools and strategies that are scientifically-proven to help you achieve your personal and career goals, whatever they may be.

Now, does that sound good?

Then let's get started...

PART 1:

SMART STRATEGIES FOR OVERCOMING BAD HABITS

CHAPTER TWO

THE SURPRISING POWER OF "I DON'T"

"A powerful agent is the right word. Whenever we come upon one of those intensely right words...the resulting effect is physical as well as spiritual, and electrically prompt."

—Mark Twain

Do you have a negative habit you want to overcome?

Or perhaps, you've decided that you're no longer going to eat dessert - a wise health choice that would cut hundreds of calories off your daily intake - and then been tempted to eat that bowl of strawberry ice cream when the waiter came over with the dessert menu?

Whatever habit you want to overcome, the simple and easy to implement technique you're about to learn in this chapter can dramatically increase your chances of achieving success.

Will this technique work 100% of the time? Absolutely not.

Will it be easy to overcome the temptations? Absolutely not.

However, the simple technique you're about to pick up *will* increase your chances of achieving success.

Imagine that you're out with friends on a hot day. You're walking about, enjoying the fresh air and getting some exercise when you stumble across an ice-cream parlor. Your friend asks, "Would you like some ice cream? I hear this place sells the best ice cream in town!"

What do you think?

Do you say to yourself:

- "I *can't* eat dessert"

or

- "I *don't* eat dessert"?

Now, I realize that grammatically, the words "can't" and "don't" are often interchangeable, especially in everyday conversations. However, psychologically, the two words have very different impacts. They subconsciously affect your thoughts and behavior very differently.

In a study that was conducted on 30 adult women who wanted to live healthier lives, some women were randomly chosen and told, "When you are tempted to skip the gym or overeat (or do anything which will hinder your health-related goal), we want you to say to yourself, "I *can't* skip going to the gym/I *can't* over-eat." Another group of the women were told to use the "I *don't*" strategy (i.e., "I *don't* skip going to the gym/I *don't* overeat").

Which group of the two do you think achieved more success? Which group do you believe managed to stick to their health-related goals - the "I can't" or the "I don't" group?

It turns out that by the end of the study, only 10% of the women who were using the "I can't" strategy had managed to use it successfully to overcome temptations to skip the gym, overeat and engage in behaviors that would negatively impact their health goals.

What about the "I don't" group? An astounding 80% of the women who were using the "I don't" strategy were using it successfully!

Think about that for a second. 10% success rate versus *80%* success rate just because of changing "I can't" to "I don't".

You might be thinking, "Come on, avoiding temptation can't be that simple! The strategy is too simple to work!"

Yes, the "I don't" strategy is very simple. However, scientific research proves that it works, so use it!

Akash P. Karia

You might be wondering, "Why is it that the words 'I don't' are more powerful than 'I can't' when trying to avoid temptation?"

Here's the explanation from the research paper published by Vanessa M. Patrick and Henrik Hagtvedt:

> We theorize that utilizing a "don't" versus "can't" refusal framing signals the degree of empowerment one has in achieving one's self-regulatory goal, resulting in a differential influence on the likelihood that we will engage in goal-directed behavior. We theorize that saying "I don't do X" connotes a firmly entrenched attitude rather than a temporary situation, and it emphasizes the personal will that drives the refusal. Thus, using the word "don't" serves as a self-affirmation of one's personal willpower and control in the relevant self-regulatory goal pursuit, leading to a favorable influence on feelings of empowerment, as well as on actual behavior. On the other hand, saying "I can't do X" connotes an external focus on impediments. We propose that this latter emphasis results in less feelings of empowerment and thus also hinders the self-regulatory goal pursuit in question."

[You can buy the full research paper here: http://bit.ly/15NOJ67]

Let me explain that in simpler language.

Think about this: When you say, "I can't eat dessert", what does it really mean? It means that there is a restriction *imposed* upon you. The restriction of not eating dessert is not your choice, but something that is being forced upon you and out of your control. It undermines your role in the decision.

However, what are you really saying when you say, "I don't eat dessert"? You're saying *you* have made a *choice* to not eat dessert - the decision comes from within you. It is of your choosing, and as a result, you're much more likely to follow through with it.

> Not only that, but the words "I don't eat dessert" become a part of your identity. Let me give you an example. I don't drink alcohol and don't smoke. I have never consumed alcohol or smoked and never will. The words "I don't" have made the decision to not drink or smoke a permanent part of my identity. Because I have repeated those words to myself over and over again, they have become part of me and affect the way I see myself. If I were to suddenly start drinking tomorrow simply because a colleague offered me some alcohol, it would shatter my image of myself and cause me unbearable pain as I try to figure out who I really am.

PRINCIPLE #1:

Instead of saying "I Can't", use the power of "I Don't"

Successful people don't do different things. They do things differently. Successful people harness the power of "I don't" when trying to eliminate negative habits from their life.

FURTHER READING

1. **"I Don't" Versus "I Can't": When Empowered Refusal Motivates Goal Directed Behavior** by Vanessa M. Patrick and Henrik Hagtvedt

Read at: http://bit.ly/15NOJ67

2. **Forbes - The Amazing Power of "I Don't" vs. "I Can't"**

"I don't is experienced as a choice, so it feels empowering. It's an affirmation of your determination and willpower. I can't isn't a choice – it's a restriction; it's being imposed upon you. So thinking "I can't" undermines your sense of power and personal agency." Read at: http://onforb.es/ZrjThy

ACTIONABLE KNOWLEDGE #1

"Bad habits are easier to abandon today than tomorrow."

—Yiddish Proverb

I highly encourage you to complete the exercises in this guide. The act of writing down your goals and plans will solidify your commitment to them. A research study conducted by Gail Matthews, PhD, a clinical psychologist at the Dominican University of California, revealed that individuals with written goals achieved approximately 50% more of their goals than those who hadn't set any clear goals.

[You can read the research summary of Gail Matthews' goal setting study here: http://bit.ly/eYj7e8]

Furthermore, answering the questions in these exercises will force you to set up concrete plans for achieving your goals and increase your probability of achieving success.

Think of a negative habit you want to change. Which negative habit is currently stopping you from achieving success? If you could eliminate one habit that is currently limiting your success, which one would it be? Write it down here:

_____

_____

_____

_____

_____

_____

Now make a commitment to stop engaging in the negative behavior. Write your commitment below using the words "I don't". For example, if your negative behavior is that you always procrastinate, write down the words "I don't procrastinate":

_____

_____

_____

_____

_____

_____

Next time you catch yourself using the words "I can't", simply replace those words with "I don't" until they become a part of your identity.

CHAPTER THREE

HERE'S WHY WILLPOWER ISN'T ENOUGH...AND WHAT TO DO ABOUT IT

"You leave old habits behind by starting out with the thought, 'I release the need for this in my life'."

—Wayne Dyer

You might be wondering, "Isn't willpower the key to avoiding temptation, fighting off cravings and achieving your goals?"

True, willpower is an essential element in overcoming temptation and making sure you consistently follow your workout plan. However, what most people don't realize is that we only have a finite amount of willpower. The more we use it, the less we have available of it.

In a classic study on willpower conducted in 1998 by psychologist Roy Baumeister, 67 study participants were led into a lab that smelled of delicious chocolate cookies. Inside the lab, some of the participants were seated in front of a table with two bowls in front of them - one bowl containing radishes and the other bowl containing delicious, freshly baked chocolate cookies.

Some of the participants were told to eat the cookies and not the radishes, and they complied happily. The others were told to eat the radishes and leave the cookies untouched. The researchers then left the room, hoping to tempt the "no-cookie" group even further.

At the end of this first experiment, researchers came back to find that the "no-cookie" group had managed to show enough self-discipline to not eat the cookies.

The participants were then asked to take part in a second experiment, which they believed was completely unrelated to the first one. They were given a logic puzzle to solve, which was actually unsolvable.

The aim of the experiment was to figure out whether using willpower would have an effect on the students' persistence when solving the puzzle. Which of the two groups do you think was more persistent when it came to solving the unsolvable puzzle?

On average, the group that had been allowed to eat cookies spent 19 minutes trying to solve the puzzle before they gave up. The "no-cookie" group, which was forced to eat radishes and use their willpower to avoid the temptation of cookies, spent an average of only less than 8 minutes trying to solve the puzzle. Why did they give up much earlier than the other group? Simple. Because they'd used up their reserves of willpower trying to avoid eating the cookies, which left them with very little willpower when trying to solve the puzzle.

This is why you might see someone who has used a lot of willpower and forced himself to go to the gym and diet every day suddenly snap and go on an eating rampage because his willpower has been exhausted.

So here's the first practical key takeaway from this study. Because willpower is exhaustible, **make sure you only set yourself only one major goal**. Don't chase after too many goals and try to change too many habits at once because doing so will exhaust your willpower and you will most likely end up achieving none of your goals.

And yes, while willpower is essential in achieving success, we also have to make sure that we use it wisely so that we don't exhaust our reserves of willpower.

This is why suppression doesn't work, because suppression uses up our finite reserve of willpower. Suppressing a craving (for example, saying to yourself: "I'm not going to eat chocolate cake! I'm not going to eat chocolate cake! I'm not even going to think about the delicious soft chocolate cake melting in my mouth!") uses up willpower. The harder you try to suppress a craving, the stronger it becomes and the more willpower you have to use to try to suppress it.

So, if suppression doesn't work in conquering negative habits, what does?

Instead of focusing on suppression, successful people focus on a replacement. Instead of trying to *suppress*, they try to *replace*.

For example, if you have the urge to eat ice cream, use the "I don't" strategy from Principle 1 and say to yourself, "I don't eat ice cream." Then, immediately begin focusing on a replacement because what you focus on gets stronger. In this case, you might begin focusing on eating a bowl of sliced fruits instead. Every time you get the urge for ice cream, replace it by eating a bowl of fruits instead. Over time, your negative habit will replaced by a much more positive one.

In his brilliant book, *The Power of Habits*, Charles Duhigg shares the story of a university student named Mandy. Mandy had a bad habit of biting her nails every time she was bored. However, her problem was much more serious than that of most people. She would bite her nails until her nails ripped away from the skin underneath. This negatively impacted her social life and her confidence.

Even with friends, she would be so embarrassed about her nails that she would become preoccupied with balling her fingers into fists or keeping her hands hidden in her pockets. She had tried very often to stop biting her nails - had tried mustering up the willpower to stop the negative habit and even painted her nails with foul-tasting polishes - but nothing had worked. Finally, frustrated with how her chronic nail biting was affecting her life, she walked into the university counseling center where she met a doctoral psychology student studying "habit reversal training".

The psychologist taught Mandy a series of steps she could take to change her habit, one of which was to immediately insert a competing response (i.e., a replacement habit) when she felt the urge to bite her nails (e.g., immediately put her hands in her pockets or grip a pencil). After a month of using this technique, Mandy's nail-biting habit had finally disappeared.

Here's another example. Let's say that you lose your temper very often. You get very angry at the littlest of things. The way to get rid of this negative habit would be to begin focusing on a replacement. So, for example, every time you get angry with an issue, you might begin focusing on taking deep breaths. By focusing on your breathing, your temper will become much easier to handle.

PRINCIPLE #2:

Don't Suppress; Replace!

Instead of trying to suppress your negative habits,
focus on a more positive replacement habit. Over time,
your negative habit will eventually get replaced with the
more positive one.

FURTHER READING

1. Fast Company - Why Change is So Hard: Self Control is Exhaustible

"Psychologists have discovered that self-control is an exhaustible resource. And I don't mean self-control only in the sense of turning down cookies or alcohol, I mean a broader sense of self-supervision—any time you're paying close attention to your actions, like when you're having a tough conversation or trying to stay focused on a paper you're writing. This helps to explain why, after a long hard day at the office, we're more likely to snap at our spouses or have one drink too many—we've depleted our self-control."

Read at: http://bit.ly/UtAxMu

2. The Limits of Willpower

Read at: http://bit.ly/IOupHK

3. Forbes - The Secret to Breaking Habits In the New Year

"Say, for example, you want to stop eating processed sweets, but you routinely have a rich dessert every night after dinner. Despite that you want to be healthier, that craving is going to come and be hard to avoid. Instead of denying it, have fresh fruit or a sugar-free alternative."

Read at: http://onforb.es/W9eyYX

4. Dr. Phil - Bad Habits and Your World

Read at: http://bit.ly/16empM9

5. News in the Health - Breaking Bad Habits: Why It's So Hard to Change

One way to kick bad habits is to actively replace unhealthy routines with new, healthy ones. Some people find they can replace a bad habit, even drug addiction, with another behavior, like exercising. "It doesn't work for everyone," Volkow says. "But certain groups of patients who have a history of serious addictions can engage in certain behaviors that are ritualistic and in a way compulsive—such as marathon running—and it helps them stay away from drugs. These alternative behaviors can counteract the urges to repeat a behavior to take a drug."

Read at: http://1.usa.gov/zF5PYp

6. The Power of Habit by Charles Duhigg

Read at: *http://amzn.to/104yQq6*

ACTIONABLE KNOWLEDGE #2

"Bad habits are easier to abandon today than tomorrow."

—Yiddish Proverb

Suppression doesn't work because it uses up too much willpower. Successful people don't focus on suppressing their negative habits, they focus on replacing them. If you want to overcome a negative habit, instead of trying to suppress it, focus on replacing it.

Write down a replacement habit (a competing response) you could begin focusing on when you have a feel an urge to do something that negatively impacts you (e.g., "When I have the urge to eat some sweets, I will immediately eat an apple instead."):

_____

_____

_____

_____

PART 2:

THE PROVEN WAY SET AND ACHIEVE YOUR GOALS

CHAPTER FOUR

JIM CARREY'S GOAL-SETTING SECRETS

"A goal is a dream with a deadline"

—Napoleon Hill

You probably know that setting a goal will increase your probability of achieving it. After all, if you don't know where you're going, how will you know when you get there? Plus, if you don't know where you're going, how will you know *how* to get there?

It's now common knowledge that setting goals can help keep you motivated. However, many people go about setting goals the wrong way. They say things like, "My goal is to lose weight" or "My goal is to become thinner" or "My goal is to look better."

These aren't goals. They are wishes! A goal is has a clear aim with a clear deadline.

The most inspiring story about the power of goal setting is that of Jim Carrey. In 1990, Jim Carrey was a struggling young comic in Los Angeles. He came from a poor family but had big dreams for himself. One day in 1990, Jim drove his old beat-up Toyota to the top of a hill. While overlooking the beautiful view, he pulled out his checkbook and wrote himself a check for $10,000,000 for "acting services rendered". He dated that check for Thanksgiving 1995.

Can you imagine the audacity of that? You're at a point in life where your dreams don't seem to be working out and you're driving a beat-up Toyota, yet here you are writing yourself a check for *ten million dollars*? He dated that check to 1995, and by 1995, he was earning $20 million...per movie!

During one of my seminars on goal setting, a participant raised an important point. He said, "I realize that it's important to set goals, but shouldn't those goals be realistic?"

It's a good point. Let me ask you a question. Do you think Jim Carrey's goal of earning ten million dollars was realistic? It may not be realistic to you, but it was realistic to *him* because he knew he had the capability to achieve it. So yes, make sure your goals are realistic to *you*, but don't let *other people* tell you what's realistic and what isn't.

The reason I told you Jim's story is not only to inspire you to set goals, but also to teach you how to set very specific goals. Notice that Jim had a very specific goal ("earn ten million dollars for acting") with a very clear deadline (Thanksgiving 1995). It was 100% clear what constituted success.

When you set a goal, make sure your goal is SMART, which stands for Specific, Measurable, Attainable, Relevant and Time-bound. Here's an example:

Specific: Instead of saying, "My ultimate goal is to lose weight," say "My goal is to lose 30 pounds."

Measurable: Set milestones to measure your progress. For example, "My goal is to lose two pounds each week."

Attainable: Your goal should be realistic to you. It should be a stretch to achieve it, but you should still feel confident in your ability to achieve it.

Relevant: This is your "why" of weight loss. Why do you want to lose weight? What motivates you? For example, your answer could be: "Achieving this goal will allow me to feel more confident as a person."

Time-bound: Set a specific date you want to achieve your goal by, e.g., "I want to lose 30 pounds by April 2014."

Once you have written down your SMART goal, make your commitment public. Share it with your friends, post it on Facebook, set up a blog on Wordpress (www.

wordpress.com) or Blogger (www.blogger.com) to share your goal and your progress with the world. Research by Gail Matthews at the Dominican University of California has shown that people who write, share and track their goals are, on average, 33% more successful in achieving their goals than those who don't.

PRINCIPLE #3:

Set a SMART Goal!

Set a SMART (specific, measurable, attainable, relevant, time-bound) goal you want to achieve. There should be no doubt about what constitutes success. After you've set your goal, share it with people who will support you in achieving it.

FURTHER READING

1. Goal Setting study by Gail Matthews

"Research recently conducted by Matthews shows that people who wrote down their goals, shared this information with a friend, and sent weekly updates to that friend were on average 33% more successful in accomplishing their stated goals than those who merely formulated goals."

Read at: http://bit.ly/voxGRZ

2. Goals: The Difference Between Success and Failure (Fast Company)

"Psychologists believe, and studies have documented, that individuals with clear, written goals are significantly more likely to succeed than those without clearly defined goals."

Read at: http://bit.ly/NxCmDu

ACTIONABLE KNOWLEDGE #3

"Goals are the fuel in the furnace of achievement"

—Brian Tracy

Successful people don't just think about what they want. They write down specific goals. People with specific goals are more likely to achieve them than people who don't set goals or whose goals are not clearly defined.

Write down your goal using the SMART principles (specific, measurable, attainable, relevant and time-bound). Make sure your goal is realistic to *you* but don't let other people dictate what's realistic and what isn't:

_____

_____

_____

_____

_____

_____

CHAPTER FIVE

HOW TO TRIPLE YOUR CHANCES OF SUCCESS WITH THIS SIMPLE TECHNIQUE

"The future depends on what you do today."

—Mahatma Gandhi

Hundreds of research studies show that the following technique can *triple* your chances of success.

Before I reveal the technique to you, let us look at one of the experiments conducted. The research study was conducted on people who wanted to exercise regularly. Some participants were told to plan when and where they would exercise each week. For example, they would plan ahead by saying, "If it's Monday, then I'll go to the gym at 5 p.m. and exercise for an hour." The other participants were given no such instructions and didn't plan ahead.

So, what were the results of the study?

It turns out that several months later, only 39% of the non-planners were exercising regularly. What about the if-then planning group? An amazing 91% of the if-then planners were still exercising regularly!

Wow, isn't that amazing? 39% success rate for non-planners versus 91% success rate for if-then planners.

Using the if-then strategy makes it much more likely that you will take action on your goals. For example, let's say that your goal is to wake up at 7 a.m. every day and go jogging. Your if-then strategy would be:

"If it's 7 a.m., I will immediately jump out of bed, put on my tracksuit and sneakers and go for a jog around the block."

The if-then strategy works because it prepares our brains for future scenarios. By planning what we will do in advance to a future scenario, we unconsciously create a mental command that tells us how to act when the said scenario arises:

- "If I feel the urge to bite my nails, I will immediately shove my hands inside my pockets."

- "If I get the craving to eat chocolate cake, then I will immediately eat some sliced fruits instead."

- "If I get angry, then I will take some deep breaths."

- "If it's a Saturday, I will go to the gym at 7 a.m.
  and exercise for an hour before having breakfast."

Now, there's one tiny warning. Don't set negative if-then goals. What are negative if-then goals? Here's an example: "If I get angry, then I won't shout." This is a negative if-then goal because it focuses on what you *won't* do, which only makes you focus more on it. It's similar to me telling you "don't think of an elephant", which of course makes you think of an elephant. Research shows that negative if-then goals can actually hamper your progress.

PRINCIPLE #4:

Use 'If-then Planning' to Triple Your Chances of Success

Set positive if-then strategy to plan how you will avoid temptations and reach your goals.

FURTHER READING

1. Implementation Intentions: Strong Effects of Simple Plans by Peter M. Gollwitzer

"An experiment by Milne, Orbell, and Sheeran (1999) investigated whether college students' participation in vigorous exercise (i.e., vigorous exercise for 20 minutes during the next week) can be increased by forming implementation intentions [if-then planning]. A motivational intervention that focused on increasing self-efficacy to exercise, the perceived severity of and vulnerability to coronary heart disease, and the expectation that exercising will reduce the risk of coronary heart disease raised compliance from 29% to only 39%. When this motivational intervention was complemented by the formation of implementation intentions [if-then planning], the compliance rate rose to 91%."

Read at: http://bit.ly/16eyGAk

2. Psychology Today - New Year's Resolution Advice You Won't Read Anywhere Else

"Use "if-then" scenarios to conserve emotional energy and triple your chances of success with hard goals. Peter Gollwitzer found that if you specify a certain cue that you will encounter during your day, and you decide what action will follow seeing that cue, you are three times more likely to be successful. Example: "When I encounter a stop sign, I will think of three blessings I have in my life." If you create this agreement ahead of time, you will not have to make a fresh decision to initiate hard behaviors, which is exhausting. Make it a foregone conclusion and save your energy for other things."

Read at: http://bit.ly/hqMoQM

3. Fast Company - Want a Simple Way to Double or Triple Your Productivity? Here's How

"A recent review of results from 94 studies that used the if-then technique found significantly higher success rates for just about every goal you can think of, including monthly breast self-examination, test preparation, using public transportation instead of driving, buying organic foods, being more helpful to others, not drinking alcohol, not starting smoking, losing weight, recycling, negotiating fairly, avoiding stereotypic and prejudicial thoughts, and better time management."

Read at: http://bit.ly/ZogBcL

ACTIONABLE KNOWLEDGE #4

"By failing to prepare, you are preparing to fail."

—Benjamin Franklin

According to research, if-then plans can help you triple your chances of success.

Write down an if-then plan to help you meet your goals. For example, "If it's 7 p.m. I will work on my novel for an hour before dinner."

_____

_____

_____

_____

_____

_____

CHAPTER SIX

HOW TO MAKE DAILY PROGRESS TOWARDS YOUR GOALS

"You are what you do, not what you say you'll do."

—C.G. Jung

A couple of years ago, I was struggling with writing a book. There were times when I would feel extremely motivated and write 30 pages of my book, and then there would be other times when I would not work on my book for months!

Have you ever had an experience like this - some days where you felt extremely motivated but then didn't work on your goal for a long period of time?

During the time when I was struggling to write, I was living in Hong Kong. It turned out that Andrew Matthews, a bestselling author of several books, was giving a seminar at one of the universities in Hong Kong. I attended Andrew's seminar and approached him at the end to ask for advice.

I told him, "Andrew, I'm struggling with writing my book. How do you manage to write so many books?"

Andrew then told me something which has changed my professional life. He said, "Akash, the secret to writing a book is to make sure you write at least one page every day, even when you don't feel like it. Write just one page every day. By the end of the year, you'll have more than 360 pages, which is the equivalent of two to three non-fiction books."

After that, I began writing a page a day. Some days, when I didn't feel like writing, I would sit down at the computer with the intention of writing one page and would end up writing over 30 to 40 pages. It was getting started that was the hardest part, but once I got started, I usually found the momentum to continue writing. Not only that, after a couple of months, writing daily became a habit and I no longer had to force myself to write because it had now become an easy habit to follow. Using this technique, I have now been able to write eight books, and I still continue writing every day.

The secret to achieving your goals is to take daily action towards them. Do one thing every day that brings you closer to your goal.

What one small action can you take every single day to get

closer to your goals? It might be to go to for a jog every day. Or it might be to spend an hour writing your novel. Whatever it is, find an action you can take daily which will help you bring you closer to your dream.

During my seminar on this topic, one of the participants asked, "I'd like to take daily action and go for a jog in the morning, but I usually procrastinate. How do I overcome this procrastination and ensure I am able to take daily action?"

The way I was able to overcome my procrastination was by having a very small goal to achieve daily - write only one page. It's such a small goal to achieve that I'm able to muster enough willpower to be able to achieve it.

I advise that you set a very small goal to achieve every day (e.g., "climb the stairs to my office instead of taking the elevator").

Another technique you can use to overcome procrastination is to utilize the five-minute technique. The five-minute technique is simply this: You spend five minutes on working towards your goal every day. For example, if your goal is to learn a new language, spend *at least* five minutes daily learning the language. Don't go to bed without having spent five minutes studying new vocabulary. Because this is such a small goal to achieve, you will always be able to muster enough willpower to achieve it.

For example, let's say your goal is to go for a jog every

morning. The idea of going for a 30-minute jog might be too intimidating and thus you might feel tempted to skip the jogging session. In this case, you can use the five-minute technique. Tell yourself, "I will go for a jog for just five minutes. Five minutes only!" Force yourself to get out of bed in the morning and go for a five-minute jog before you come back and get into bed.

Usually, you will find that if you get started working on your goal for five minutes, you will become so immersed in it that you will spend 20, 30 or even 60 minutes on it. You might get up with the intention of going for a five-minute jog and end up jogging for an entire hour because you've overcome the hardest part of getting started. Yes, on some days, you might manage nothing more than just a five-minute jog, which is fine because you've still met your daily goal and made some progress. Most importantly though, the five-minute technique establishes a habit - a habit where you continually work on your goal - where you go for a jog every single day. Within several months of using the five-minute technique every day, you will be able to stop relying on willpower and rely instead on the power of habit to go for a jog.

If the five-minute technique doesn't work for you, set an even smaller goal. For example, let's stick to the goal of going for a jog. Let's say that you feel so demotivated in the mornings that you don't even want to go for a five-minute run. In that case, you can set yourself a goal of just getting up and putting on your tracksuit and sneakers.

That's it. Just wake up and tell yourself, "I'll just put on my tracksuit and sneakers, and then go back to bed!" Usually, once you've put on your tracksuit and sneakers, the power of momentum will carry you forwards and you will end up going for a short jog. However, on other days, you might literally manage just to put on your tracksuit and sneakers before you go back to bed, which is fine because at least you're setting the foundation for a positive habit.

PRINCIPLE #5:

Create a Healthy Habit by Taking Daily Action

Commit yourself towards taking some form of daily action to achieve your goals. Use the five-minute technique to help you overcome procrastination. Make sure you spent at least five minutes every day making progress towards your fitness goals. Eventually, you will be able to rely on the power of habit to help you achieve your goals.

FURTHER READING

1. FitWatch - Seven Important Steps to Setting Your Weight Loss Goals

"Create a very detailed, daily action plan that you can follow. This is important because there won't be any questions or confusion about what to do each day – you'll be able to see it in black and white. Commit to it. Read over your plan and make a solemn commitment to stick to it no matter what."

Read at: http://bit.ly/pHCLuH

ACTIONABLE KNOWLEDGE #5

"Productivity is never an accident. It is always the result of a commitment to excellence, intelligent planning, and focused effort."

—Paul J. Meyer

Commit yourself to taking daily action to achieve your goal.

Write down one small action you can take every single to day to get closer to your dream (e.g., "If it's 7 a.m. then I will go for a ten-minute jog around the park").

_____

_____

_____

_____

_____

_____

Utilize the 5-minutes-per-day technique or set an even smaller goal (e.g. "get out of bed and put on my tracksuit") to make sure you take daily action.

CHAPTER SEVEN

THE BEST WAY TO KEEP TRACK OF YOUR PROGRESS

"If you're walking down the right path and you're willing to keep walking, eventually you'll make progress."

—Barack Obama

Keeping track of your progress is an important step towards achieving your goal. It's important that you hold yourself accountable in some way - by having a friend keep tabs on your progress or by monitoring your progress yourself (e.g., by putting a tick on the calendar every time you take action towards your goal).

Keeping track of your progress has other benefits too. By seeing how far you have come (called *"to-date thinking"*), you will feel encouraged by the progress you have made. At the same time, seeing how far you have left to go (called *"to-go" thinking*) will motivate you to do more.

51

While both to-date thinking and to-go thinking are beneficial, is one more beneficial than the other?

In a study conducted at the University of Chicago by psychologists Minjung Koo and Ayelet Fishbach, 92 undergraduate students studying for exams were split into two groups. The first group was told they had already covered 48% of the course (to-date thinking) and the other group was told they had 52% of the course still left to cover (to-go thinking). 48% left to go and 52% already covered is the exact same thing, just framed differently.

However, do you think there was a difference in the motivation levels of the two groups of students?

It turns out that students who had to-go thinking (the ones who were told they had 52% of the material still left to cover) were more motivated than the students who used to-date thinking (the ones who were told they had covered 48% of the course).

Why is this? This is because when you use to-date thinking (e.g., "I've written two chapters today!"), your brain celebrates its little victory. You feel a sense of accomplishment, the way you would if you had actually finished the *entire* task. Your brain relaxes and motivation decreases while you bathe in the glow of your accomplishment.

However, when you use to-go thinking (e.g., "I still have two more chapters to write!"), your brain focuses on the end goal. Like a sprinter who focuses on the finish line, your brain channels its effort and focus on the end goal, making you more motivated on finishing the entire task.

PRINCIPLE #6:

Use "to-go" thinking to keep yourself motivated

While both to-date and to-go thinking have their benefits, having too much to-date thinking can hinder your progress. Yes, when you are feeling uncommitted to your goal or feeling you lack confidence to achieve your goal, celebrate the milestones you reach to motivate you. However, if you are committed to your goal - which I know you are because you are reading this book - make sure you use to-go thinking to focus on the end goal to increase your motivation.

FURTHER READING

1. **Dynamics of self-regulation: How (un)accomplished goal actions affect motivation** by Koo, Minjung; Fishbach, Ayelet

"We found that to-date (vs. to-go) information increased the motivation to study for a course to which participants were not committed. Therefore, these participants followed a dynamic of highlighting; that is, they chose to study because they had completed some coursework.

In contrast, to-go (vs. to-date) information increased the motivation to study for a course to which participants were committed. Thus, they followed a dynamic of balancing; that is, they chose to study because they had remaining coursework that they had not yet completed."

Read at: http://bit.ly/15UCJzI

2. Harvard Business Review Blog - How to Become a Great Finisher

"Koo and Fishbach's studies consistently show that when we are pursuing a goal and consider how far we've already come, we feel a premature sense of accomplishment and begin to slack off."

Read at: http://bit.ly/kzHeTr

3. Self Influence - Common Advice Scientifically Proven to Kill Motivation

"Those thinking about how much work was left to do studied less and reported feeling less motivated. Those thinking about how much work they'd accomplished felt more motivated and studied for more hours. Researchers say this is because when you think in terms of how much progress you've made on something important to you, it activates a drive to achieve more balance, so you end up spending more time on other goals."

Read at: http://bit.ly/qS7c5B

4. Ten Reasons You Should Keep a Fitness Journal

"It keeps you accountable. When you are answering to the pages, you are stuck with the reminders to your commitments."

Read at: http://aol.it/11MA2Q7

5. Men's Health - The Mind Trick that Motivates You

"According to a recent study from the University of Chicago, thinking "I have 10 minutes left of my workout"—not "I've been doing this for 20 minutes"—can help you reach your target faster. Your move: Break your big goals, like losing 10 pounds, into mini goals. Aim for a pound a week, then once you get closer to the 10, focus on the small amount you have to go."

Read at: http://bit.ly/OZoiDt

ACTIONABLE KNOWLEDGE #6

"You don't make progress by standing on the sidelines, whimpering and complaining. You make progress by implementing ideas."

—Shirley Chisholm

Find an accountability partner who will keep track of your progress to your goal. Write the name of your accountability partner below:

_____

_____

_____

_____

_____

_____

Find a way to monitor your progress regularly (daily, weekly, monthly). For example, you can put a tick on a calendar every time you take action towards your goal. Alternatively, you can write in a journal to monitor your progress. Write down how you will monitor your progress regularly:

_____

_____

_____

_____

_____

_____

When you lack confidence in your ability to achieve your goal or you are feeling uncommitted towards achieving your goal, use "to-date" thinking to motivate yourself. In other words, remind yourself of how much you have already achieved. This will put you in a positive frame of mind and drive you to achieve it.

_____

_____

_____

_____

_____

_____

For people who are confident in their ability to reach their goal and are committed to achieving it, using to-go thinking increases motivation. Make sure you keep your eyes set on the final prize (to-go thinking) to ensure that your motivation and focus stay high.

_____

_____

_____

_____

_____

_____

CHAPTER EIGHT

HOW BEING A REALISTIC OPTIMIST HELPS YOU ACHIEVE MORE SUCCESS

"I always look on the optimistic side of life, but I am realistic enough to know that life is a complex matter"

—Walt Disney

Have you watched the documentary, *The Secret*? If you haven't watched it, *The Secret* talks about the key to achieving anything you want in life: visualizing whatever it is that you want as though it is already in your life. For example, if you want to lose weight, all you have to do is close your eyes and visualize a thinner, sexier you. Visualize your wonderful, flexible new body. Feel the happiness and pride you would feel about having lost weight. Keep visualizing and sending out positive vibrations into the universe until the universe rewards you with your new, sexy body.

I know I'm about to step on a lot of toes and hurt a lot of people's feelings in this chapter by saying that the path to success outlined in *The Secret* might not work.

I'm not saying that *The Secret* is entirely wrong. In fact, science has shown that visualization - as advocated in *The Secret* - helps increase your chances of achieving success. Personally, before I give a speech or conduct a seminar, I visualize myself delivering the talk from start to finish and making a positive impact on the audience. This helps increase my confidence and puts me in a positive state of mind. When I am in the gym, I visualize my muscles growing bigger as I lift weights, which motivates me to keep lifting. So go ahead and visualize. Visualize your goals and dreams because there are positive benefits of visualization.

However, I believe that the part where *The Secret* does unintentionally mislead people is in making people believe that success is easy to achieve: Simply visualize your goals, send your positive intentions into the world and the Universe will reward you with whatever you desire. This mentality of "success is easy to achieve" can be detrimental to your success. And this isn't just my opinion - it's backed up by solid scientific research.

In a weight loss study conducted by psychologist Gabriele Oettingen, a group of obese women were asked how confident they felt about reaching their goals. Some of the women said they were very confident whereas the others said they doubted their ability to achieve their weight loss goals.

The results? Unsurprisingly, the women who said they were confident they would succeed lost 26 pounds more than the self-doubters.

This is an expected result. If you're confident in your ability, you're much more likely to work harder and be motivated to achieve your goal than if you kept doubting yourself.

However, here's where the study gets interesting. The women were also asked how easy they thought their road to success would be.

The results? The women who said that their path to success would be difficult lost 24 pounds more than women who thought they would succeed easily.

What this shows is that while confidence is a good thing because it makes it more likely you will meet your weight loss goals, believing that the process of losing weight will be easy can hinder your success.

The best way to achieve success is to be confident in your abilities while also expecting that you will face difficulties on your journey towards achieving your goal. Don't visualize success coming easily. Instead imagine the obstacles you will encounter and visualize yourself persisting even in the face of those difficult obstacles.

For example, when I visualize my seminars, I don't expect that the seminar to be flawless. I realize that things that will go wrong: my PowerPoint slides might not display correctly, the microphone might stop working or the audience might not get my joke. I visualize myself tackling these challenges and as a result, when these challenges do arise, I am prepared to handle them without losing my confidence.

PRINCIPLE #7:

Be a Realistic Optimist

Be an optimist, but a realistic one. Be confident in your ability to achieve success. However, be realistic about the process - realize that it won't be easy. Prepare yourself for the difficulties you will encounter and visualize yourself persisting even when things get rough.

FURTHER READING

1. **Expectation, fantasy, and weight loss: Is the impact of positive thinking always positive?** By Gabriele Oettingen and Thomas A. Wadden

"We investigated the impact of expectation and fantasy on the weight losses of 25 obese women participating in a behavioral weight reduction program. Both expectations of reaching one's goal weight and spontaneous weight-related fantasies were measured at pretreatment before subjects began 1 year of weekly group-treatment. Consistent with our hypothesis that expectation and fantasy are different in quality, these variables predicted weight change in opposite directions. Optimistic expectations but negative fantasies favored weight loss"

Read at: http://bit.ly/Yh5dUz

2. Men's Health - The Mind Trick that Motivates You

"For more than 10 years, social psychologist Gabriele Oettingen, Ph.D., has studied different methods of visualization and goal-attainment. Here's what she's figured out: Simply imagining your goal—such as exercising more often, or eating better—is more likely to drain your energy than to inspire you. Why? Positive fantasies don't include the hard work and effort needed to make a change or reach a goal, Oettingen says. And so, when you're faced with those real-life roadblocks, your fantasy falls apart and you tend to feel demoralized."

Read at: http://bit.ly/OZoiDt

ACTIONABLE
KNOWLEDGE #7

"Being in control of your life and having realistic expectations about your day-to-day challenges are the key to stress management, which is perhaps the most important ingredient to living a happy, healthy and rewarding life."

—Marilu Henner

People who are confident about achieving their goals are more likely to achieve them than self-doubters. How confident are you about achieving your goal? Make sure you set a goal that you are confident about achieving. It should be hard to achieve, but you should still be confident in knowing that if you work hard enough, you can achieve it.

_____

_____

_____

_____

_____

People who realize that success will not come easily are more likely to achieve success than people who think success is easy. What difficulties and obstacles do you think you will encounter on your path to success? Write those obstacles below and write how you might handle them:

_____

_____

_____

_____

_____

_____

Visualize yourself not just achieving success, but also persisting in the face of difficulties.

PART 3:

PREPARING FOR AND HANDLING FAILURE

CHAPTER NINE

WHAT AN EXPERIMENT ON SIXTH-GRADERS CAN TEACH YOU ABOUT SUCCESS

"Don't be afraid to fail. Don't waste energy trying to cover up failure. Learn from your failure and go on to the next challenge. It's OK to fail. If you're not failing, you're not growing."

—H. Stanley Judd

Building on the principle of realistic optimism, successful people don't just anticipate obstacles, they also anticipate failure. They realize that the journey to their dream is full of failures to learn from, and so they give themselves permission to fail. Thus, when they do encounter rejection and failure, instead of giving up, they keep on working towards their dream because they see failure as a part of the process.

In her 2008 Commencement Address at Harvard, J.K.Rowling, author of the mega-bestselling *Harry Potter* series, which was rejected 12 times before it was published, said, "It is impossible to live without failing at something, unless you live so cautiously that you might as well not have lived at all, in which case, you fail by default."

For Thomas Edison, the famous American inventor, failure was an essential step of innovation. He failed *ten thousand times* before he finally managed to invent the light bulb. On the topic of failure, he said, "Results! Why, man, I have gotten a lot of results! I know several thousand things that won't work." The reason Thomas Edison was able to persevere in the face of failure was that he had given himself permission to fail.

Whatever goal you are trying to achieve, whether it's starting up a business, losing weight or doubling your income, it's likely that you will encounter some form of failure or rejection. Just like a young child falls hundreds of times when trying to ride a bicycle, it's likely that you too will fall in the pursuit of your goal. Have you given yourself permission to fail?

Experiments conducted by French researchers back up the claim that giving yourself permission to fail actually improves performance. In one experiment, 111 sixth-graders were given difficult anagram problems. A select group of the students were told that the learning could be challenging and that they might sometimes fail. Other students were given the "it's-okay-to-fail" talk.

The results of the experiment were that the group which was told it's-okay-to-fail did *better* than the group that hadn't been given permission to fail. Why? Probably because the students who had been given permission to fail felt less pressure to perform perfectly and thus felt free to try out different problem-solving methods when one method didn't work.

So, what's the takeaway for you? If you want to be successful, then go ahead and give yourself permission to fail.

PRINCIPLE #8:

Give Yourself Permission to Fail

By giving yourself permission to fail, you receive the same benefits: you release yourself from the pressure to succeed immediately and are more likely to keep persevering when you do fail.

FURTHER READING

1. Improving Working Memory Efficiency by Reframing Metacognitive Interpretation of Task Difficulty by Frederique Autin and Jean-Claude Croize
Read at: http://bit.ly/YH1SR2

ACTIONABLE KNOWLEDGE #8

"Do not brood over your past mistakes and failures as this will only fill your mind with grief, regret and depression. Do not repeat them in the future."

—Sivananda

Write a letter to yourself giving yourself permission to fail. Tell yourself that it's okay to fail as long as you are willing to get back up and continue trying.

_____

_____

_____

_____

_____

_____

Give yourself some buffers so that you don't feel demotivated when you do fail, but commit yourself to not using those buffers unless you really must.

_____

_____

_____

_____

_____

_____

CHAPTER TEN

THE MAGIC OF MINDSET

"Identify your problems, but give power and energy to your solutions."

—Anthony Robbins

Do you think people's intelligence, talents and abilities are fixed or can they be changed?

Your answer to that question can dramatically affect your success in life, so think about that question carefully.

Carol Dweck, Stanford Professor and author of *Mindset: The New Psychology of Success*, has conducted decades of research showing that there are two types of mindsets: fixed mindsets and growth mindsets.

A person with a fixed mindset is someone who believes that their abilities are fixed. They believe that they have a certain amount of talent and that's it. As a result, they avoid challenges because they don't want to risk failing. They see view failure as a negative judgment of their abilities. They reject criticism and negative feedback – even when it is useful – because they regard it as a criticism of themselves instead of their abilities. They regard effort as fruitless because, after all, if they have to put in effort to achieve success, it means they're not intelligent enough.

A person with a growth mindset is someone who believes that their intelligence and abilities can be trained. They readily embrace challenges because they view challenges as an opportunity to improve themselves and develop new skills. Furthermore, because their self-image is not tied to their successes, they view failure and negative feedback as an opportunity to learn. They view effort as a necessity in improving their skillset. Their self-image is tied to how much effort they put in, not whether they succeed or fail. Instead of trying to prove how good they are, they focus on getting better.

Which one of the two mindsets best describes you?

Do you believe your abilities are fixed or can they be developed through effort?

Do you stick to doing things you know or do you take on new challenges even though there is a possibility you will fail?

Do you view failure as a negative judgment of your abilities or as an opportunity to learn?

Is your self-image tied to your intelligence or to your effort?

It's not surprising that people with growth mindsets are people who achieve the most success in life. Because they believe their abilities and skills can be developed over time, they invest in themselves by attending seminars, reading books, seeking out mentors. Because they are not concerned with proving how smart they are, they take on new challenges and persist in the face of failure – which eventually leads them to achieve success.

So, how do you develop a growth mindset?

The good news is that now that you know the difference between the two mindsets, you can *consciously* make a decision about which mindset you want to adopt.

When you get the opportunity to take on a new challenge or opportunity, instead of feeling threatened by the prospect of failure, boldly *choose* to take on the challenge. Consciously choose to view the challenge or obstacle it as a learning opportunity.

When you find yourself wanting to prove how smart or talented you are, snap yourself out of that mindset. Instead, focus on how much effort you're going to put in. Instead of rewarding yourself for your successes, take pride in how much effort you put it – even when you do fail.

When you fail on your journey to your goal, instead of

thinking, "I'm not good enough", replace that inner dialogue with, "What did I learn from this? How much better am I now because of this experience?" Doing this isn't easy, but when you do start viewing failure as a learning opportunity, you will develop a growth mindset which will ultimately achieve success.

When I first started competing in public speaking contests, I had a fixed mindset. I was focused on giving the perfect speech and impressing the judges and the audience with my impressive speaking skills. I felt proud of my ability to win speech contests even though I had written my speech the previous day whereas my competitors had been practicing for months.

When I did lose, I would become demotivated because I felt that the loss proved that I was not good enough. I would vow never to take part in any more speech contests because "the judges didn't know what they were talking about!" When audience members gave me feedback on how to improve, I would reject their advice because I viewed it as an attack on my ability. As a result, I missed out on a lot of opportunities to improve myself as a speaker.

After discovering the research on mindsets, I took asked myself which mindset I had and made a conscious decision to have a growth mindset. Instead of viewing my speaking ability as being fixed, I began viewing it as a skill that could be developed with effort. I began valuing the effort I put into writing and practicing my speeches instead of focusing on whether I won or lost. Ironically, this mindset helped me win a lot more success as a speaker than did the fixed mindset. I began asking audience members how I could improve my speeches because I no viewed negative feedback as an attack on my ability. Using this growth mindset, I was able to learn more about the art of public speaking in two months than I had in the previous two years.

A study conducted by Carol Dweck and Lisa Blackwell showed that it's possible for us to change from a fixed mindset to a growth mindset, and that doing so can have great impact on your success. In the study, low-achieving seventh graders were split into two groups. One group attended a study-skills session on how to improve their memory. The other group attended a session which taught them that intelligence, like muscle, can be developed through exercise.

The results of the study were shocking. Students who attended the memory-skills sessions showed *no improvement*. However, the students who were taught to adopt the growth mind-set – to view challenges and failures as learning opportunities – had increased motivation and received better grades.

Knowing the research on mindsets, train yourself to adopt the growth mindset. Every time you find yourself falling into the fixed mindset, snap yourself out of it and make a conscious decision to adopt the growth mindset.

> ### PRINCIPLE #9:
>
> ### Adopt a Growth Mindset
>
> Approach your goal, any negative feedback and any failures, through the lens of a growth mindset.

FURTHER READING

1. **Mindset: The New Psychology of Success** by Carol Dweck

Read at: http://amzn.to/11XCZPW

ACTIONABLE KNOWLEDGE #9

"Today, you have the opportunity to transcend from a disempowered mindset of existence to an empowered reality of purpose-driven living. Today is a new day that has been handed to you for shaping. You have the tools, now get out there and create a masterpiece."

—Steve Maraboli, The Power of One

People with growth mindsets view challenges, negative feedback and failure as learning opportunities. Research shows that it's possible to adopt the growth mindset simply by making a conscious decision. When you find yourself falling into the fixed mindset, consciously choose to adopt the growth mindset instead.

_____

_____

_____

_____

_____

CHAPTER ELEVEN

WRAP UP: HOW SUCCESSFUL PEOPLE THINK DIFFERENTLY

"The starting point of all achievement is desire."

—Napoleon Hill

We've covered a lot of tools and techniques for achieving success in this tiny book. This chapter will serve as a useful summary of some of the most important tools and techniques covered in the book.

1. When trying to overcome temptations, successful people think "I don't" instead of "I can't".

2. Successful people don't think about what they don't want. Instead, they think about what they *do* want.

3. Instead of suppressing negative habits, successful people focus on replacing them.

4. Instead of vaguely thinking about what they would like to achieve, successful people write and share SMART goals.

5. Successful people use "if-then" thinking to achieve their goals. Using "if-then" planning triples their chances of achieving success.

6. Successful people commit themselves fully to their goal and take daily action to achieve it.

7. Successful people use the five-minute technique to overcome procrastination.

8. "To-go" thinking keeps successful people motivated so that they can achieve their goals.

9. Unsuccessful people think that achieving their goals will be easy. Successful people are confident in achieving their goals but realize that the process of doing so will be difficult. If you want increase your chances of achieving your goals, be a realistic optimist.

10. Successful people don't just visualize success. They also think about and prepare themselves for the difficulties they will encounter. They visualize themselves persisting even when things get rough.

11. Successful people think of failures as part of the process of achieving success. Instead of shying away from failure, they give themselves permission to fail.

Doing so allows them to still stay motivated even when they do fail.

12. Unsuccessful people think that their abilities and intelligence levels are fixed. Successful people think that they can improve themselves through hard work.

13. Unsuccessful people look at criticism and failure as a negative judgment of their abilities. Successful people, on the other hand, view criticism and failure as opportunities for improvement.

14. Successful people are successful because they make a **conscious choice** to adopt the above habits, attitudes and thinking processes. Success is not an accident - **it is a choice.**

QUESTIONS OR COMMENTS?

I'd love to hear your thoughts. Email me at: akash.speaker@gmail.com

INTERESTED IN HAVING ME SPEAK AT YOUR NEXT EVENT?

I deliver high-impact keynotes and workshops on productivity, time-management, success psychology and effective communication. Check out the full list of my training programs on http://AkashKaria.com/keynotes/ and reach me on akash.speaker@gmail.com to discuss how we can work together.

GRAB $297 WORTH OF FREE RESOURCES

Want to learn the small but powerful hacks to make you insanely productive? Want to discover the scientifically proven techniques to ignite your influence? Interested in mastering the art of public speaking and charisma? Then head over to http://www.AkashKaria.com to grab your free "10X Success Toolkit" (free MP3s, eBooks and videos designed to unleash your excellence). Be sure to sign up

Akash P. Karia

for the newsletter and join over 11,800 of your peers to receive free, exclusive content that I don't share on my blog.

OTHER BOOKS BY
THE AUTHOR

If you enjoyed this book, then check out Akash's other books (and see what other readers are saying).

Ready, Set...PROCRASTINATE! 23 Anti-Procrastination Tools Designed to Help You Stop Putting Things off and Start Getting Things Done
"This is one book you should not delay reading! Having struggled with procrastination for much of my life, Akash Karia's book came like a breath of fresh air. He provides clear, practical advice on how to overcome the problem, but warns that you will need to work at it daily. This is a quick, very useful read and with 23 tips on offer, there will be several that you can identify with and implement for immediate results. If there is just one thing that you should not put off, it is reading this book."

— Gillian Findlay

Get the book on Amazon:
http://AkashKaria.com/AntiProcrastination/

ANTI NEGATIVITY: HOW TO STOP NEGATIVE THINKING AND LEAD A POSITIVE LIFE

"Akash is a master at taking complex ideas and communicating with simplicity and brilliance. He honors your time by presenting what you need to know right away, and follows up with some excellent examples as reinforcement. If you're looking for some simple and effective ways to stop thinking negatively and a new season of positivity, definitely check out this book."

— Justin Morgan

Get the book on Amazon:
http://AkashKaria.com/AntiNegativity/

PERSUASION PSYCHOLOGY: 26 POWERFUL TECHNIQUES TO PERSUADE ANYONE!

"I'm a huge fan of Akash's writing style and the way he can distill quite a complex subject into concise bite-sized points you can take away and convert into action. The book covers many different aspects of persuasion from the way you look to the words you use."

— Rob Cubbon, author of
"From Freelancer to Entrepreneur"

Get the book on Amazon:
http://AkashKaria.com/Persuasion/

HOW TO DELIVER A GREAT TED TALK: PRESENTATION SECRETS OF THE WORLD'S BEST SPEAKERS

"Why can some speakers grab the attention of an audience and keep them spellbound throughout their entire presentation, but most fall flat on their faces and are quickly forgotten? Akash has captured the best ideas, tools, and processes used by some of the best speakers and presenters in the world. *He has distilled them in to a step-by-step, easy-to-read guide that will help you discover, develop, and deliver presentations which help you stand out from the crowd... Whether you are a new speaker learning the art of speaking, or a veteran looking for a new perspective, How to Deliver* a Great TED Talk is a wise investment that can help take your speaking to a higher level."

— Michael Davis, Certified World Class Speaking Coach

Get the book on Amazon:
http://AkashKaria.com/TEDTalkBook/

WANT MORE?
Then check out Akash's author page on Amazon on http://bit.ly/AkashKaria.

ABOUT THE AUTHOR

Akash Karia is an award winning speaker and peak-productivity coach who has been ranked as one of the Top Ten speakers in Asia Pacific. He is an in-demand international speaker who has spoken to a wide range of audiences including bankers in Hong Kong, students in Tanzania, governmental organizations in Dubai and yoga teachers in Thailand. He currently lives in Tanzania where he works as the Chief Commercial Officer of a multi-million dollar company.

"If you want to learn presentation skills, public speaking or just simply uncover excellence hidden inside of you or your teams, **Akash Karia is the coach to go to**." — *Raju Mandhyan, TV show host, Expat Insights, Philippines*

"Akash Karia is a fine public speaker who knows his subject very well. He has an immense understanding in what it takes for a successful presentation to pull through. **A rare talent who has much in store for you as an individual, and better yet, your organization**." — *Sherilyn Pang, Business Reporter, Capital TV, Malaysia*

Voted as one of the "**10 online entrepreneurs you need to know in 2015**" by *The Expressive Leader*

Featured as one of the "**top 9 online presentations of 2014**" by *AuthorStream.com*

Akash is available for speaking engagements and flies from Tanzania. Contact him for coaching and training through his website: www.AkashKaria.com

CPSIA information can be obtained at www.ICGtesting.com
Printed in the USA
LVOW11s2057050916

503292LV00005B/172/P